M000011732

AN IDEAS INTO ACTION GUIDEBOOK

Selling Yourself Without Selling Out

A Leader's Guide to Ethical Self-Promotion

IDEAS INTO ACTION GUIDEBOOKS

Aimed at managers and executives who are concerned with their own and others' development, each guidebook in this series gives specific advice on how to complete a developmental task or solve a leadership problem.

LEAD CONTRIBUTORS	Gina Hernez-Broome
	Cindy McLaughlin
	Stephanie Trovas
CONTRIBUTORS	David Baldwin
	Jessica Baltes
	Suzanne Ernster
	Sue Lundberg
	Eric Roth
DIRECTOR OF ASSESSMENTS, TOOLS, AND PUBLICATIONS	Sylvester Taylor
MANAGER, GLOBAL PUBLICATION DEVELOPMENT	Peter Scisco
EDITOR	Karen Lewis
WRITER	Rebecca Garau
DESIGN AND LAYOUT	Joanne Ferguson
CONTRIBUTING ARTISTS	Laura J. Gibson
	Chris Wilson, 29 & Company

CCL No. 431
978-1-882197-95-8

CENTER FOR CREATIVE LEADERSHIP
WWW.CCL.ORG

AN IDEAS INTO ACTION GUIDEBOOK

Selling Yourself Without Selling Out

A Leader's Guide to Ethical Self-Promotion

Gina Hernez-Broome, Cindy McLaughlin, and Stephanie Trovas

TM
Center for
Creative
Leadership®

THE IDEAS INTO ACTION GUIDEBOOK SERIES

This series of guidebooks draws on the practical knowledge that the Center for Creative Leadership (CCL®) has generated, since its inception in 1970, through its research and educational activity conducted in partnership with hundreds of thousands of managers and executives. Much of this knowledge is shared—in a way that is distinct from the typical university department, professional association, or consultancy. CCL is not simply a collection of individual experts, although the individual credentials of its staff are impressive; rather it is a community, with its members holding certain principles in common and working together to understand and generate practical responses to today's leadership and organizational challenges.

The purpose of the series is to provide managers with specific advice on how to complete a developmental task or solve a leadership challenge. In doing that, the series carries out CCL's mission to advance the understanding, practice, and development of leadership for the benefit of society worldwide. We think you will find the Ideas Into Action Guidebooks an important addition to your leadership toolkit.

Table of Contents

EXECUTIVE BRIEF

High-performing individuals and groups are often not adequately recognized for their contributions. The antidote to being overlooked or underestimated is self-promotion—the act of generating personal visibility in service of your work and career. In this guidebook, we discuss how you can benefit from self-promotion *and* maintain your integrity and authenticity. We help you reframe common beliefs that get in the way of effective self-promotion, and we provide numerous strategies and activities that can become part of your repertoire.

Self-Promotion: A Leader's Job

Andrew is employed by a large auto parts manufacturing company. He leads a team that investigates new ways of solving his division's order-processing mishaps. Through careful analysis, Andrew's team finds that the system is not plagued with problems; rather, the employees who use the system are not adequately trained. As a result, people do not have a uniform understanding of how the system operates.

Within weeks, the problem is corrected and client satisfaction begins to increase. Andrew decides to bring his team's discoveries to the next company-wide meeting. His intent is to showcase the good work of his team, but his decision to share has far greater impact. Other divisions of the company discover that they have the same problem and can implement similar solutions. Eventually these efforts lead to an 18 percent improvement in processing time for the company.

The work of Andrew's team had a large impact on the organization. But those benefits could have easily been overlooked for months or years if Andrew had not talked about his team's accomplishments. Andrew and several members of the team also garnered personal benefits from their actions. Andrew moved to the short list of executives slated to head up a new overseas division. Others on his team were recommended for key positions or project teams.

The purpose of self-promotion is to gain visibility for the contributions you and your group make to the organization. When used intentionally and strategically, self-promotion can be rewarding for individuals as well as the organization. Many leaders expect visibility and recognition to result from doing good work, but simply doing good work may not be enough to achieve those

---

A Necessary Evil

In 2005 CCL surveyed a number of participants from several of its development programs to get their thoughts on the practice of self-promotion in the workplace. The survey data confirmed the tension leaders often express: Self-promotion is usually associated with bragging, showing off, or selling out. At the same time, self-promotion is seen as important for career success and for influencing others. This perception that self-promotion is a necessary evil prevents leaders from becoming effective self-promoters. They don't do it well, don't do it consistently, and don't view it as a positive and useful aspect of leadership.

---

results. Self-promotion is an additional component that creates visibility and communicates value, and thus it is an essential part of being a leader. Creating visibility for yourself and your group is part of your job. It is a key to effectiveness and long-term success.

Strategic Visibility and Its Benefits

Self-promotion is a way to honestly leverage the accomplishments, strengths, and skills of individuals or groups. Think of effective self-promotion in terms of strategic visibility, meaning that you are intentional in the way you publicize, what you share, and—most important—how you communicate. Leaders who have developed an effective technique of creating visibility do so in a pattern that is credible, consistent, and sincere. When approached with authenticity and integrity, self-promotion helps to build the valuable social capital needed to accomplish business outcomes.

8

Benefits for the Individual

The visibility created by effective self-promotion has benefits for the individual leader. Promoting yourself and your group is an effective way to enhance your career. Certainly, self-promotion may advance your career over time in terms of pay and promotion. It will help you to get what you've worked for and deserve. It also provides many enhancements to your work life along the way, including the following:

Rewarding opportunities. Challenges, increased responsibility, chances to meet or work with different people—these types of opportunities can be interesting and rewarding.

Recognition and reward for your contributions. Acknowledgment is a great motivator. And when you are motivated, you can more readily develop and sustain a commitment to the organization and your work.

Confidence. Taking risks, becoming more visible, and trying new things can be a challenge, but doing so will only build your confidence. Putting yourself out there allows you to build on your strengths and develop new skills—key experiences for growth as a leader.

Increased self-worth. When you're valued by others for your contributions and capabilities and gain experiences that build your confidence, your overall sense of self-worth is enhanced.

Credibility. Trust is largely built on credibility. Both traits are difficult to earn and very easy to lose. Effective self-promotion helps you earn the confidence of others for your ability and expertise: technical skill, communication style, ability to hone in on the heart of an issue, and so on. Authentic self-promotion helps to ensure that your reputation matches your accomplishments. Consistent and appropriate self-promotion makes you a known commodity; people know what to expect from you. With credibility you have the ability to motivate, to inspire, and to be worthy of others' trust.

Influence. Much of the work in today's organizations involves persuading, negotiating, and seeking buy-in. Your ability to influence others is, in many ways, tied to what others think of you. If you are seen as ineffectual, isolated, lacking in confidence, or limited in knowledge or expertise, you will have little influence compared with others who are viewed as effective, well connected, powerful, knowledgeable, and up-to-date. Self-promotion is a way to inform others about what you bring to the table. When others are open to your influence, you can negotiate for scarce resources, generate support, affect organizational decisions and outcomes, and gain access to crucial people and information.

Benefits for Others

It's not all about you, of course. When it comes to touting their work, leaders should think beyond their personal interests. Self-promotion is also about your obligations to others.

Direct reports. You have a responsibility to advocate and create opportunities for your direct reports to grow and be successful. When you show your boss an article published by a group member or talk about a supervisor's quick thinking on the production floor, you are demonstrating several things: You have talented people in your department. You have respect for the contributions of others. You are a leader whose people should be noticed.

Boss. Don't expect your boss to know you are doing a good job. Make it easy for your boss to be your advocate and to use you and your group as examples of what she is doing right. Let her know about your accomplishments, what's going well, what your strengths are. When you update your boss about the value of a new tracking system or report on how you finessed a tough negotiation, you're giving her information she needs to do her job, keep an accurate view of her talent pool, and generate visibility for her group.

Group. Being willing and able to promote yourself is a way of enrolling others in the excitement and energy of the work. Whether you are a group leader or among a group of peers, you can foster pride in the group and its work when you willingly share recognition, opportunities to learn, and visibility in the organization. When, for example, you encourage another group member to give the presentation to your boss, you are publicly showing that you value the group and its contributions.

Organization. The organization deserves to have the right person in the right job. It also deserves to gain maximum benefit from the activities, information, and ideas that are generated by its talent pool. When you keep quiet about your skills and accomplishments, when you downplay your role, when you keep information to yourself, you are limiting yourself and the organization. Redundancies and conflicts will be hidden, opportunities for collaboration will be bypassed, and valuable information won't be fully leveraged. You may be overlooked for a job or role in which you could make a great contribution.

Rethinking Self-Promotion

Many leaders are not comfortable with the concept and practice of self-promotion. It is often viewed with derision—as a personal public-relations campaign, a way of shouting "Look at me! I'm the best!" Even leaders who see the value of self-promotion are often unsure how to proceed.

Many of us have beliefs or mind-sets that get in the way of effective self-promotion. As a result, many talented managers avoid promoting themselves, their work, and their groups. Unfortunately, they and their organizations are missing out on the benefits of greater visibility.

To overcome your hesitancy or aversion, it is helpful to understand common barriers to effective self-promotion. We call these *limiting beliefs*. If you can find a new perspective, or reframe your belief, you'll find that self-promotion will become more natural and more effective.

Limiting belief: **Accomplishments should speak for themselves.**
Reframed: **A lot of good work falls under the radar.**

Many, many people believe they shouldn't have to promote themselves because good work will speak for itself. Or they believe that meeting the requirements of the job ("I'm just doing my job. What is there to promote?") will provide sufficient visibility. Unfortunately, this is not true. Many managers are surprised to find that bosses, peers, and direct reports do not recognize their skills and contributions. It is your job to let people know about your work, why it is important, and how it benefits others. Never assume that you will be noticed, given credit, or rewarded for your accomplishments if you don't share them. Don't assume the grapevine will work in your favor either; you need to communicate with all of your stakeholders.

Limiting belief: **Productivity trumps promoting.**
Reframed: **Promoting is productive.**

Promoting yourself and your group is part of your job. If you want to be truly productive, you need to shift your mental model

What's Your Promotional Personality?

Can you spot your behaviors and reactions in one of the descriptions below?

SCHMOOZER. You are highly social and know everybody. You like to see and be seen, particularly with "the right people."

Your challenge: Make sure that you are not perceived as a phony with little substance and a big agenda. Your interactions should be meaningful and genuine with everybody. *New mind-set:* Self-promotion should be targeted, intentional, and sincere.

WORKER. You are highly competent, work oriented, and productive. You view social activities, networking, and self-promotion as time wasters.

Your challenge: Expand your view beyond the task and take a broader view. See how connections enable you to have stronger impact. *New mind-set:* Self-promotion contributes to workplace effectiveness.

ANTI-BRAGGART. You see self-promotion as bragging and obnoxious and will go to extremes not to be perceived that way. Overly modest, you often deflect praise and are quick to take blame.

Your challenge: Ensure that your skills and your work are viewed and valued accurately by others. Stop downplaying your contributions. *New mind-set:* There's a difference between bragging and authentic self-promotion.

SELECTIVE MARKETER. You know the value of self-promotion and have had some positive experiences as a result of touting your work, your group, or your talent. Even so, you are unsure of how to consistently or strategically market yourself without overdoing it.

Your challenge: Integrate self-promotion into your routine work and communication so that it is appropriate, useful, and consistent. *New mind-set:* Self-promotion is an ongoing leadership task, not an occasional activity.

away from seeing it as a waste of time. Instead, look at it as a way to sell yourself as a resource to the organization. Your productivity will not be jeopardized; in fact, it will improve when you have the information and the relationships to get the resources, information, and support you need.

Limiting belief: **Who has the time?**
Reframed: It's part of the job.

Many people say they don't have the time to talk up their work. To reframe this view, consider ways that effective self-promotion could save time in the long run for you and your group. When you talk about your efforts and your successes, you create an opportunity to prevent redundant work. When people in the organization are unaware of what others are doing, they spend time on tasks and projects that are unnecessary. Promoting your work opens the door to greater access to the people and information needed to integrate, collaborate, and put energy where it counts.

Limiting belief: **My boss is too busy to hear me talk about myself.**
Reframed: My boss is so busy he needs my self-promotion.

Isn't it part of your boss's job to know what's happening in the department? By keeping your boss informed, by providing the information he needs, you are, in fact, doing your job. Your very busy boss doesn't want to have to pry things out of you: tell him what is going well, where the struggles are, what you need. If your boss is informed, he won't be blindsided. Communication builds trust, rapport, and relationships.

Limiting belief: **Team players don't take credit.**
Reframed: Visibility benefits the team.

Perhaps you're part of a corporate culture that values the group over individual effort. Or maybe you've been burned by others taking credit for your work. Whatever the reason, if self-promotion seems in conflict with your group orientation, then it's important to equate self-promotion with group benefits. We're not advocating claiming credit for work or ideas that are not yours; we are saying that high visibility benefits the group. You need to be skilled at communicating the value of the work and the talent of the people in the group. At times, your efforts may highlight your individual role; in other cases you may promote another group member or the group as a whole. This type of promotion generates support, information sharing, cooperation, and resources, as well as rewards and recognition for a deserving group.

Limiting belief: **Senior management doesn't want to hear about me.**
Reframed: **Senior management appreciates both information and talent.**

Effective self-promotion isn't all about you—but it is about your leadership role. While senior management does not need excruciating detail about you and your current task, they do want to know that you are engaged in your work and in the goals of the organization. Have a clear statement in mind—a promotional sound bite—about a key project or component of your work. If you're asked about your work, you can take advantage of the moment to demonstrate your credibility as a communicator and a leader. For instance, if someone asks, "How is your project?" don't limit your response to "It's fine" or "We're really busy." Instead say, "The project is great," and then briefly describe what you've done so far and how it's making a difference.

Limiting belief: **I don't want to brag.**
Reframed: **I need to inform.**

Of course nobody likes braggarts—obnoxious coworkers who think way too much of their talents and will talk up their

15

accomplishments and importance at every opportunity. And while sometimes people with voice and visibility succeed without substance, more often success comes from substance that is skillfully illuminated. Talking about your work, your successes, the value of your group, and so forth does not require braggadocio. Shift your mental model: you need to inform others to get buy-in and gain attention for the success of the business. Talk about your accomplishments as a way to help others who might be working on similar projects or task forces. Again, sell yourself as a resource to whatever project or product. One great way to do this is to take on a visible job—the position creates the opportunity and the need for you to let people know what you're doing. Think of it as walking into the spotlight rather than trying to shine it on yourself.

Limiting belief: **Only schmoozers go to company events.**
Reframed: Company events are opportunities to make a connection.

Company meetings, trade shows, receptions, and other events are often lost opportunities. Rather than viewing them as unnecessary or unpleasant, think of events as simply your chance to make a connection. You don't need to network relentlessly or corner the VP to discuss your latest project. Think ahead about the people you might want to talk to, everyone from the executive you barely know to the group member you haven't worked with for a year, and plan what you might want to say. Ask questions—find common ground on which to make a connection. Listening is often more important than talking. What can you find out that will help you?

Limiting belief: **I'm not interested in playing politics.**
Reframed: Knowing the political landscape is necessary and productive.

Many people believe that only those who don't have the skills to do their jobs need politics. In fact, CCL research has shown that many people believe that getting ahead in their organizations results from skill at politics, as opposed to performance. So given that organizational political systems are alive and well and that sometimes people do get promoted based on their ability to work the political system, how can you compete on a performance basis alone? First of all, *politics* does not have to be a bad word. Playing the political game or using politics to override poor performance is not the only way to be politically savvy. Think about politics in terms of knowing the relationships and cultural dynamics of the organization so that you can be more effective on the job. Then you can use politics as a tool for understanding the landscape of work and responding to that reality. Remember that you were not hired to work in a vacuum. You have to understand the people, the structure, and the currents of organizational life in order to know what will work for you as a leader.

Limiting belief: **I'm very uncomfortable promoting myself.**
Reframed: I can promote myself in a way that is effective and maintains my integrity.

For a variety of reasons, some people are incredibly uncomfortable speaking up about their accomplishments. This discomfort may be stronger in people with introverted or quiet personalities, those who don't have any interest in being in the spotlight, or those who see self-promotion as conflicting with their values. For leaders who naturally shy away from self-promotion, the key is to use tactics and behaviors that are effective and, at the same time, will maintain a sense of integrity and authenticity. For example, leaders who are uncomfortable touting their accomplishments are well served by the buddy system: finding a colleague who has a similar struggle and finding ways to give recognition to and promote each other. By pitching each other, you'll gain benefits associated with greater visibility for your work while getting practice in the art of touting the work.

Techniques for Promoting Yourself

Choosing the techniques that suit you and your situation best is an important step toward effective and authentic self-promotion. Connecting with people and taking advantage of opportunities using suitable behaviors help individuals develop the skills to promote themselves in comfortable and influential ways. We've grouped the techniques into three categories: connecting with others, developing yourself, and creating opportunities.

Connecting with others addresses strategies and tactics that help you build your network, create relationships, and gain visibility in the organization. Developing yourself focuses on skills and behaviors that are useful in your efforts to promote yourself. Creating opportunities is about the where and when of self-promotion—specific actions that lend themselves to visibility and self-promotion.

In real life, the categories often overlap. In fact, in your efforts to become more skilled and more comfortable with self-promotion, you will want to address all three areas in some fashion. For example, you might choose to be more proactive (developing yourself) in your efforts to make your boss aware of your ability to resolve conflict (connecting with others). You could volunteer to lead a group to address a challenge that involves competing agendas and opinions (creating opportunities).

Connecting with Others

This category includes strategies and tactics that help you build your network, create relationships, and gain visibility in the organization.

- **Cross-pollinate.** Sometimes the best ideas come from unexpected sources. Allow more people to be an ongoing part of your team, initiative, or problem-solving process. You can draw on their information, expertise, and experience.

- **Extend an invitation.** Invite people from other areas of the business to sit in on a meeting to give a fresh perspective. An "outsider" may have useful ideas and information to share, or may simply stimulate good discussion. You may also discover common concerns and find ways to work together or share resources.

- **Involve senior people.** To get noticed and implemented, many good concepts need a person with formal authority or a high degree of influence. Ask seasoned or senior people for their insights and opinions. Once they've given their input, you have a good reason to keep them informed.

- **Ask for help.** One of the simplest and often overlooked ways of making useful connections is to ask for help. By asking for other people's assistance, you naturally have to describe your work. They may not have known of your involvement in a project, and this gives you a sincere way to talk about your work.

- **Spread the word.** Communicate with a wide group of stakeholders. Present a project to a group that has a link to your work. Describe the positive results and the obstacles you've overcome. You may have solved an issue that other people are just tackling. If you share your accomplishments, they won't have to reinvent the solution.

- **Communicate up.** Ensure that management is aware of and understands results achieved and special accomplishments. Put your best foot forward in meetings with management.

- **Acknowledge collective effort.** When you promote yourself, be sure to recognize the group that helped make you successful. Touting the accomplishments of your group is one of the most comfortable ways to gain visibility, extend your network, and build relationships.

- **Recognize individual contributions.** Give praise and credit to specific individuals for good work.

- **Model self-promotion.** Set the standard for the group to talk about their work. Modeling effective self-promotion sets a positive tone and shows specific behaviors for others to emulate.

- **Seek opportunities for group members.** Ask other group members to make presentations or attend meetings where your project may be discussed.

- **Celebrate visibly.** When you have a success, don't keep the news under wraps. Celebrate your group's accomplishments in a way that invites others to find out more. Create an awards ceremony, host a party, put up signs, give out T-shirts, or spread the news via e-mail or the company newsletter.

- **Promote your boss.** You are on your boss's team. Apply your group-promoting mind-set to your boss's priorities and interests.

- **Give feedback.** Tell your boss what you think. By providing your boss with appropriate feedback, you are setting an appropriate tone of openness. This will provide you more opportunities to talk about your own contributions, share your ideas, and generally build a stronger relationship.

- **Talk action and results.** Find a way to tell your supervisor about your efforts and successes on a regular basis. A structured update in a staff meeting, routine e-mail, or weekly report may work for you. Or your practice may be to inform as you go—communicating news when it occurs.

- **Connect to the boss's view.** What are your boss's priorities, goals, needs, and challenges? Try to link your work to what the boss has in mind.

- **Educate your boss.** Find ways to share a new skill, a new system that you have set up, or a new business idea or article. Make your boss smarter, more informed.

- **Prepare for performance reviews.** If you've been communicating with your boss on an ongoing basis, your performance review becomes an opportunity to summarize or frame your skills and areas for improvement. Prepare and plan so you can use the review to highlight what matters most to you: what you have accomplished, what you would like to do next, areas for development. Just as you would prepare for a job interview with a potential boss, pull together your thoughts and information for your review.

- **Create a promotional partnership.** Become an advocate for a peer and have that person do the same for you. Choose your partner carefully, of course. That person's credibility becomes tied to yours.

- **Keep your partner in the know.** Update and inform your partner about your work and successes, but also keep him or her updated about your goals for self-promotion. If your partner knows you're seeking a project to work on with senior management, for instance, he or she can keep an eye out for suitable opportunities.

- **Tap into your partner's world.** Use his or her networks to access others and raise visibility for yourself, your work, and your group. Through regular activities, your partner may be able to tout your efforts in ways that would be inaccessible to you directly.

- **Reciprocate.** Be your partner's biggest fan. Find ways to promote his or her skills and successes. Of course, always be genuine and knowledgeable in your advocacy.

Developing Yourself

This category focuses on skills and behaviors that are useful in your efforts to promote yourself.

- **Be honest and open.** Self-promotion isn't about putting out false or exaggerated information. It is about being honest, genuine, and frank about your work and your efforts. Talk about the results, but also about how you achieved them.

- **Acknowledge the positive.** In your routine discussions and meetings, be sure to talk about successes, what is working well, and what is on track. If you think only in terms of challenges or frustrations, you and others will fail to see the successes and the positive aspects of the work.

- **Don't ignore trouble spots.** Effective self-promotion requires that you recognize challenges and problems. Otherwise, your credibility will suffer. Another benefit: Your trouble areas may be just the key to new relationships and visibility. For example, you might say something like this to a peer who asks about your current work: "We've come a long way in key areas, but now we're struggling with _____. In fact, you may be just the person I need to talk to. We could really use help/ideas/input from someone with your experience/perspective."

- **Learn to summarize.** People are too busy to notice all you do, much less make important connections or understand the implications. It is part of your job to communicate and inform. Find ways to summarize, edit, and package your work (think in terms of newspaper headlines). Formal and informal presentations for executive management need to be especially well prepared and succinct.

- **Be proactive.** What are your needs and interests for the short term and long term? Let your needs and interests be known. Plant the seeds for future opportunities and connections. Don't wait around for someone to hand you good opportunities to shine. If you don't ask, someone else probably will, and you'll miss out.

- **Practice your pitch.** Develop an elevator speech about yourself. Create one for every key project. Think through key points so that you will be prepared and poised when given a chance to tell others about your role.

- **Plan ahead.** Can you answer the question "Where do you want to be in three years?" If not, you need to take time to reflect and get clarity. You can then seek out the experiences, skills, and relationships you need to get there. When you have a chance to talk with a senior person in the organization, you can present yourself as goal oriented when you say something like "Leading the cross-functional team is giving me great experience. It will prepare me to take on more responsibility in the future."

- **Collaborate.** Bring others in early on in a process. Let them know what you are trying to achieve and explain benefits for stakeholders. Then work collaboratively to develop ideas and solutions. In other words, getting people engaged generates buy-in and makes implementation go more smoothly. When it comes to self-promotion, this approach gives you visibility and credibility, and helps build relationships.

- **Connect with a need.** Consider your audience and find ways to connect with their needs. Proactively listen to people on any concerns or suggestions. What are you doing that affects them or benefits them? Do you have a shared need? Promoting yourself can be a win-win when you understand others' points of view.

- **Highlight past wins.** Remind others of past successes by making a link to similar current circumstances. If you have effectively trained a group of new employees with a new process, offer to apply that knowledge and experience to departmental training on a new computer system.

- **Be clear about I versus we.** When others are taking credit personally for joint accomplishments (whether consciously or not), don't accept it. It may seem like a minor point, but it isn't. Take action: it may mean giving feedback to a peer or jumping in and adding your contributions.

- **Know the political landscape.** It is important to understand the workings of the organization: Who are the people you need to know? What does it take to get things done? How does the system work? When do you need to follow the system, and when can you work around it? Understanding the organization is key to effective leadership. When you have a good understanding, you can better determine how, when, and how much self-promotion is appropriate.

- **Value all levels.** Don't forget about people in lower ranks in the organization. People you've worked with in the past or people whose positions are often underappreciated can be important sources of ideas and information. They can help you understand the landscape, and you can help them get recognition.

- **Don't hoard information.** The more you release information, the more powerful it becomes. Don't hoard or hold on to it. Share the information as much as you can with as many people as makes sense. What makes sense? You will know if you know the political landscape you are in.

Creating Opportunities

This category is about the where and when of self-promotion—specific actions that lend themselves to visibility and self-promotion.

- **Find the forum.** Take opportunities in public forums (group or staff meetings) to diplomatically report on accomplishments, achievements, milestones, and successes you are genuinely proud of.

- **Practice strategic visibility.** Pick and choose your message and your audience. A well-timed "verbal advertisement" can go a long way.

- **Step into the spotlight.** Take on challenging work assignments or high-visibility projects. If the project is highly visible, you have a better chance of getting noticed. Make your projects visible to management and ask for opportunities to present what you've done to specific groups that can benefit.

- **Allow yourself to shine.** Be sure to accept the credit when credit is due.

- **Take charge.** Be assertive and take charge when given an opportunity to lead, especially in high-profile situations.

- **Use your routine.** Lunches, breaks, and informal gatherings are the routine activities that help you make connections on a personal level. You don't need to be touting your work; think of it as relationship building.

- **Pass on the positive.** Good news and compliments from satisfied customers, clients, direct reports, peers, and others are worth passing on. Forward those e-mails to your boss. If people give you compliments, ask if they would mind taking a moment to let your boss know. Keep your own file of compliments—they make a good read when you need a boost and a good resource at performance review time.

- **Showcase your strengths.** What are your skills? In what situations are you confident? Seek opportunities to interact with senior management in situations that showcase your strengths.

- **Volunteer for visibility.** Volunteer for opportunities and responsibilities that put you in a position of visibility. By signing up, you communicate a positive, confident self-image. Plus, you get good experience.

- **Create a moment.** Come up with your own event. Host a speaker and invite people from other departments to attend. Propose an award for an important achievement, manage the process, and be the one to present the honors. Set up a lunch group with one or two other persons, with the rule that each must bring someone else for the group to get to know.

- **Choose—and use—your events.** You don't need to attend every employee function, and you certainly don't need to "work the room" every time. Identify one or two people you would like to meet or speak with. An easy approach is to attend corporate social events that you are genuinely interested in. For example, if your corporation holds a charity event, you may enjoy the chance to give to your community. But you'll also benefit from the interaction with people outside your immediate work group.

- **Join an industry association.** Get involved with organizations related to your work. You can bring in fresh ideas and new relationships to bear on your work. You may even gain kudos or recognition by the association, giving you another opportunity to promote your value and expertise.

Finding the Sweet Spot

For leaders, self-promotion is a key component to effectiveness and long-term success. But like most behaviors, it can be overdone or underdone to their detriment. To develop strong, effective self-promotional skills, leaders need to find the sweet spot between over-the-top, obnoxious bragging and being overly modest and overlooked.

To find the sweet spot, stay focused on the value of the work. Don't let your mind-set prevent you from doing this. Take yourself out of the equation . . . even though you will gain and benefit. By focusing on the work itself, you will not go overboard with bragging, nor will your hesitancy to be in the spotlight become a liability.

Suggested Readings

Browning, H. (2012). *Accountability: Taking ownership of your responsibility.* Greensboro, NC: Center for Creative Leadership.

Bunker, K. A., & Wakefield, M. (2005). *Leading with authenticity in times of transition.* Greensboro, NC: Center for Creative Leadership.

Collins, J. (2001). *Good to great: Why some companies make the leap . . . and others don't.* New York: HarperBusiness.

Deal, J. J. (2007). *Retiring the generation gap: How employees young and old can find common ground.* San Francisco: Jossey-Bass.

Goleman, D., Boyatzis, R., & McKee, A. (2002). *Primal leadership: Realizing the power of emotional intelligence.* Boston: Harvard Business School Press.

Grayson, C., & Baldwin, D. (2007). *Leadership networking: Connect, collaborate, create.* Greensboro, NC: Center for Creative Leadership.

Hoppe, M. (2006). *Active listening: Improve your ability to listen and lead.* Greensboro, NC: Center for Creative Leadership.

Kaplan, R. E. (1999). *Internalizing strengths: An overlooked way of overcoming weaknesses in managers.* Greensboro, NC: Center for Creative Leadership.

King, S. N., Altman, D. G., & Lee, R. J. (2011). *Discovering the leader in you: How to realize your personal leadership potential* (New and Rev. ed). San Francisco: Jossey-Bass.

King, S. N., & Altman, D. G. (2011). *Discovering the leader in you workbook.* San Francisco: Jossey-Bass.

Scharlatt, H. (2008). *Selling your ideas to your organization.* Greensboro, NC: Center for Creative Leadership.

Scharlatt, H., & Smith, R. (2011). *Influence: Gaining commitment, getting results* (2nd ed). Greensboro, NC: Center for Creative Leadership.

Background

Our attention was drawn to the role of self-promotion in our work with participants in CCL programs and in our experience as coaches for clients. Oftentimes, participants in our CCL leadership programs are surprised when they learn, through 360-degree feedback, that their bosses and peers view them as less effective than they see themselves. That brings up the question of whether they need to improve key skills or if they just need to improve their ability to communicate, or promote, those skills.

The drawbacks to keeping quiet in an organization are also revealed through CCL's Looking Glass Experience (LGE). In the program, participants go through a business simulation. Repeatedly, we've seen participants who have valuable information and know the most falling short as leaders and team players. By holding back, they limit the organization and themselves.

Finally, when the subject of self-promotion as a leadership skill comes up among program participants and coaching clients, it invariably sparks a discussion about the negative side of self-promotion.

To better understand people's views and behaviors around self-promotion, we analyzed several sources:

- survey data from clients and program participants

- program experience as coaches and faculty

- review of 360 assessments comparing self, boss, and direct report data

- problem and issue questionnaire administered in LGE (data compares information known, decision making, influence, and effectiveness)

- case studies

Key Point Summary

The purpose of self-promotion is to gain visibility for the contributions you and your group make to the organization. When used intentionally and strategically, self-promotion can be rewarding for individuals as well as the organization. Many leaders expect visibility and recognition to result from doing good work, but simply doing good work may not be enough to achieve those results. Self-promotion is an additional component that creates visibility and communicates value, and thus it is an essential part of being a leader. It is a key to effectiveness and long-term success.

The visibility created by effective self-promotion has benefits for the individual leader. Promoting yourself and your group provides many enhancements to your work life, including pay and promotion, rewarding opportunities, recognition and reward for your contributions, confidence, increased self-worth, credibility, and influence. Your self-promotion efforts can also have benefits for others: your direct reports, your boss, your group, and your organization as a whole.

Many leaders have beliefs or mind-sets that get in the way of effective self-promotion, and as a result, avoid promoting themselves, their work, and their groups. Unfortunately, they and their organizations miss out on the benefits of greater visibility. To overcome your hesitancy or aversion, it is helpful to reframe your limiting beliefs.

Techniques for promoting yourself include connecting with others, developing yourself, and creating opportunities. Connecting with others addresses strategies and tactics that help you build your network, create relationships, and gain visibility in the organization. Developing yourself focuses on skills and behaviors that are useful in your efforts to promote yourself. Creating opportunities is about the where and when of self-promotion—specific actions that lend themselves to visibility and self-promotion.

To develop strong, effective self-promotional skills, leaders need to find the sweet spot between bragging and being overly modest. To do so, stay focused on the value of the work. By focusing on the work itself, you will not go overboard with bragging, nor will your hesitancy to be in the spotlight become a liability.

Ordering Information

To get more information, to order other Ideas Into Action Guidebooks, or to find out about bulk-order discounts, please contact us by phone at 336-545-2810 or visit our online bookstore at www.ccl. org/guidebooks.

Printed in the USA
CPSIA information can be obtained
at www.ICGtesting.com
LVHW080834080124
768037LV00027B/82